THEM'S YOUR MAMMY'S PILLS

and other poems

First published 2015
The Dedalus Press
13 Moyclare Road
Baldoyle
Dublin 13
Ireland

www.**dedaluspress**.com

Editor: Pat Boran

Copyright © Leland Bardwell, 1991, 2006, 2015

ISBN 978 1 910251 08 9

All rights reserved.
No part of this publication may be reproduced in any form or by any means without the prior permission of the publisher.

Dedalus Press titles are represented in the UK by
Central Books, 99 Wallis Road, London E9 5LN
and in North America by Syracuse University Press, Inc.,
621 Skytop Road, Suite 110, Syracuse, New York 13244.

The Dedalus Press receives financial assistance from
The Arts Council / An Chomhairle Ealaíon

THEM'S YOUR MAMMY'S PILLS
and other poems

LELAND BARDWELL

DEDALUS PRESS
DUBLIN, IRELAND

EDITOR'S NOTE

These poems were originally published in two Dedalus Press volumes, *Dostoevsky's Grave: New & Selected Poems* (1991), long since out of print, and *The Noise of Masonry Settling* (2006). Minimal changes have been made to the text, and then only to correct errors or inconsistencies in spelling or punctuation.

Contents

Dostoevsky's Grave (1991)

Obituary for Leland Bardwell / 11
Housewife / 12
For Paul and Nessa / 13
They Put a Bed in the Passage / 15
Sailor Song / 16
Husbands / 18
On Being Shut Out of Desmond O'Grady's
Flat in the Small Hours / 19
Wife Waits for Husband / 20
Inishbofin / 22
An Afternoon with The Artist
at The Quinn Club / 24
Inishbofin (The Roue) / 26
Mother Said It Would Be All Right
When Frances Came / 27
Outside The Odeon, Camden Town / 32
Before Going Up / 33
First / 34
Crybaby / 35
Snow Love / 36
How My True Love and I Lay Without Touching / 37
From a Painting by Artemesia Gentileschi / 38
Chain Strokes / 39
Exiles / 40
Remembering the Blindness of Jorge Luis Borges / 43
Breach Baby / 44
Pointless / 45
Clondalkin Concrete / 46
Moth Dust / 47

Children's Games / 48
Her Sister's Child / 50
After Pushkin / 51
Memory / 52
On Mistaking a Jesuit Lecture for a Poetry Reading / 53
Lion / 55
Dostoevsky's Grave / 56
In Memoriam John Jordan / 57
Dawn Guest / 58
Brother / 59
History Stopped That Night / 60
Letter to my Teacher / 61
Note / 63
CT Scan / 64
A Single Rose / 65
Roses / 66
The Price of Shoes in Russia / 67
The Bingo Bus / 69
Lila's Potatoes / 71
Them's Your Mammy's Pills / 73
An Unusual Irish Summer / 75
Kassia / 76
Skipping Banville in Barcelona / 75
Maggie's Cottage / 78

THE SOUND OF MASONRY SETTLING (2006)

The Knowledge of Beezie McGowan / 81
Moving House / 82
'These Aspirins Seem To Be No Use' / 83
I'll Do the Messages / 84
Hard to Imagine Your Face Dead / 85
For Dermot and Anne Marie
on Attending the Birth of Dallan / 86

Where the Grass is Dark with Trees / 88
Lobster Fishing / 89
Oh Well! *(de mortuis ... etc)* / 91
The West's Asleep / 92
That Day / 93
Office Vignette / 94
My Brother Reggie / 95
Love Poem / 96
The Night's Empty Shells / 97
Heart Trouble / 98
Innismurray / 100
We Don't Serve Travelling People / 101
'No Road Beyond the Graveyard' / 102
Hawthornden Castle / 104
Drum Up a Poem / 105
Cherry Blossom Again / 106
Old People's Outing: Ageism / 107
Block / 108
The Lady Who Went on Strike Outside The Iveagh Hostel Because of its Early Closing Hours / 109
Ghost Child Runs / 110
The Grave-digger / 112
A Paean for My Uncle Kit Who Died Before I Was Born / 113
The Ballad of the Fisherman's Wife / 116
Innocents / 117
Bag Lady / 118
Barnacles / 119
Insomnia / 120
Pigeon Outside the Dead Woman's House / 121
Maugherow Movements / 122
The Invisible, from the USA to Iraq / 123
The Song of the Whale / 124
We Sell, You Buy: Gulf War 1 / 125
S.A.D. / 126
The Horse Protestant Joke is Over / 127

House for Sale / 128
Song / 129
In the Out-Patients of St. Mary's Hospital,
On the Eve of Good Friday Last / 130
'The Act of Poetry Is a Rebel Act' / 131
Precisely / 132
Prison Poem III / 133
Prison Poem IV / 134
Two Poems i.m. Stevie Smith / 135
The Bed Bug / 136
In My Darling Liza's Eyes / 137
Four Woodbines / 138
Mrs. Katherine Dunne, Street Trader,
Camden Street, Dublin, Died March 1983 / 139
Nightmare / 140
A Mother Mourns Her Heroin-Addicted Daughter / 142
The Violets of the Poor / 144
Black in Achill / 145
Megan Fair Remembered, 1977 / 146

Dostoevsky's Grave

Obituary for Leland Bardwell

Lea-land – there was no shelter there;
no shelter from the cutting North.
So she went North into the brume.
For a while the new broom swept clean
but then the ashes of her bed
soon turned to rust
And there was cold.
The earth was a frozen lump.
North again she went into the further
doom where the map ends
and she remembered the South
where the strollers were
like Mandarin figures on a Chinese silk;
"Have I come too far?" she asked
an old man making masks.
But he was waspish and unkind;
he answered not but pointed with skinny hand
to Lea-land – there was no shelter there.

Housewife

They filled in the halo
with chalk
a better picture, this,
they thought
(for she's no saint.)
They put pebbles on her nipples
to weigh them down.

She feigned patience;
    she waited,
        waited,
            waited.

Occasionally, during the waiting period
she came up with a small truth
while sweeping the dust
off the bread; at first
there was fruit, and left-overs
to finish up; soon
the water even was gone,
and money was everything.

Then the panther came
and sat on her lap.
His paws created a diversion
as soft as mushrooms on her thighs.

They tried to send her away
but she sat still.
(They knew there'd be a toll
for her returning,

But that would be later
much later.)

She was crouching now,
her breasts lay naked on her ribs
like cotton gloves,
her legs had got like daffodil stalks
but her eyes were still angry.

The panther had gone.

The only way she knew this
was by the tone of their voices.

The way they could tell she was still there
was by the noise of the cupboard doors
being opened and shut.
She must be looking for something,
they said.

For Paul and Nessa

on the occasion of their marriage

Apart, they tore the ropes asunder
and, clearing the decks, each
cast a net in his own turbulent mind;
there revealed a high solitude
as equivocal as a war to end wars;
cast again for certainty, and found
memories old as an ill-tuned drawing room piano;
cast again for beauty and found
the petals of asters,
each petal as thin
as a strand of the future.

They shall weave with the petals of asters
the skin of a shirt.

They Put a Bed in the Passage
ON FIRST LOOKING INTO ST. PAT'S

for John Jordan

They put a bed in the passage
and said "lie down".
Glory glory glory
to the spring, not this side
of Thomas Street.
For we don't believe in flowers.

They gave us the dark side of the moon
to live upon
and not content with that
they quartered it till
it looked like a bad banana.
There we clung together
as far apart as possible
till the others came.
They brought ichor in their syringes
these dark venal furtive earth-men
and we admired them,
like we admired Messrs. Stafford, Young and Cernan,
but we didn't envy them.

For they shall return whence they came
like landlords who get no rent.
We promised to pay the rent
and we believed it. But we didn't do it.

That's why they kept coming back.

Sailor Song

i.m. Commander Robert Cooper

My great-uncle Bob went French
and spoke of *naufrages* –
he had traded sailors like silk
in foreign parts.
He showed me 'Beetlejuice',
the brightest of all Orion's mates.

    The night sky spins on the lever
    the mariners love – it's a nervous sea.
    The Leeward Islands lift and dip,
    the sailors are braced by a nip of rum.
    Is it spikenard that wafts through the smothering fog?
    (The seabed lifts as the cormorants dive.)

With the drift of years the waves
must have arched their backs to flatter
the sailor who scanned his vegetable plot,
the furcoated caterpillar swung
on the cabbage leaf.
(The Red Admiral pinned to the box
was a butterfly hoax.)
It was strange that an old old man should have jet black hair.

    I feared that he would fall or drop
    a priceless porcelain jar – I feared
    he would trip on the crusty stair
    and a carved wood head would bounce and chip,
    but I never feared that he would die.

Only part of the heart's equipped
for a legacy of empty rooms –
a telescope to read the sky,
the lingering camphor smell
in the empty butterfly box.

Husbands

My first husband hated intelligent women –
he thought they were like avocado pears,
expensive, tasteless.

He said if I was let loose
I might go to Mexico
although his horizons
were leather skirts.

My second husband hated Mexicans
and me. He said we had ended the transfer.
He liked Antonioni women
with short hair and big bums
and wanted to be one.

I'd like a new one with no hatreds
and superb teeth.
Both my husbands had grey smiles
and were transvestites.

I thought that stupid.
(So what if my breasts
are like two fried eggs?
They haven't any.)

I was once screwed in Euston Station
and saw mercury running.
If I could have bottled it
I'd have made a fortune.

On Being Shut Out of Desmond O'Grady's Flat in the Small Hours

Was it for this we crossed the Rubicon
(the crazy monk on roller skates)
Dove il scuola Athenaeum?
(a thousand Japs in the Vatican)

Amor dapis means *amor lacrimarum*
Legal organic high –
(There are nettles by the Tiber,
they are wet, they sting.)
Non sunt fiori.
And thou shalt weep
upon the water.

With the small annoyances of dawn –
a lost key –
il Professore sleeps
with his halo askew.

We'll play peripheral giants
and tell half the story.

Wife Waits for Husband

Why do you come wine-dressed
with your whisky kisses
and throw back my curtain
wanting my ripples?

I do not lie corsetted
there is no toll-gate
come crazy come weary
but do not come wine-dressed
with your whisky kisses

turn over tiredly turn
the bed over
tell me I'm whoring
tell me I'm wrong
but don't come with
tresses don't come with weeds
the dandelion clock
is the maker of seeds

he loves me he loves me
he loves me   not lately

but do not come wine-dressed
from botchy night glories
do not come wine-dressed
with mother-made stories

come with the whisky
and give me to drink
the future is fox-glove
it's poison it's poison
but poppy will soften
the lines on my street.

Inishbofin

Mikey's eyes see further than the long sea
    in the short bar.
If an island is another land it isn't Ireland
and the islanders' insulated laugh is a valediction
    that no partings fathom.

Yet we return again and again
    as the pleated sea swells
to allow ourselves that moment of joy
as the *Melody* docks, the crafty old engines
    grinding to a halt
and Mikey's cagey welcome, small drops of merriment
waltzing in the irises
would make the Twelve Bens bow down in salutation.

His brother Christy rests athwart the bows
    (he never smiles).
His salt lips are dried by his daily death
    banging from port to port with cargo and caution.
His melody is the song he sings when the sun
    dips over the island's spine.

The rest of the crew, Young Jim, in his forty years
    a stranger to both, harbours his eyes
    like the skin of the bog where the sun runs like a scythe.
Languid and orderly in his labour he hurls
    the Guinness kegs on the harbour tip.
Short shrift for the returning vagrants
    from Kensal Rise or Ealing West
or the Johnnie-come-latelys like ourselves
    gratefully settled like plovers on motionless ground

while the crowd disperses and the island, a figure of eight,
    subsides once more in its ocean bed.

Mikey, stately in his sixty years,
    drifts to Day's Bar, leaving the future behind him.

An Afternoon with The Artist at The Quinn Club

for Gerry Mangan

Pat Quinn is the plenipotentiary
of compassion – like the blue whale
he puffs and gurgles, gurgles and puffs.
While the cloves of hot spirit
cluster his lips, he spreads vines
on the tampered marrow-skin,
the monastery of his seventh child.

The dusk made a twist of lemon in a furtive sky.
Damp winter settled on the Wicklow night.
sealed the little episodes of mud
with slate thin ice – the children repaired
with effortless confusion
to the thud of the pinball tables.

Free mandarin roots for all
roll up somnambulists, the empire is yours
we are the great sharers
something for all the family.
The ticket man has braced his varicose heart,
has adopted a surgeon's smile.
He knows the camels of fortune
don't come to poets. When the knees
swell and mottle like turnips
they'll yell for the knife.

The artist drinks his vodka straight –
we toast – all centuries combine –
the supreme and wide dominion –
the year of the Tiger.

We listen carefully to the cushions.

Inishbofin (The Roue)

In the hot roar of Murray's bar
The Roue stares lustfully
the old trench-coat hardened
like asbestos –
catch as catch can –
on the way to the toilet

We're crazy about this place
of wild mint and garlic,
imagine poems can solve everything,
grow into the landscape
like the surface turf
or like adding polish to a shoe.

But The Roue is there
sanding his lust in the blind way
we trip in ruts on a moonless night –
if he goes home empty
with his limping dog
we lie untouched
among the nameless grave stones.

Mother Said It Would Be All Right When Frances Came

Mother said it would be all right
when Frances came.

Since the consumption took Rose
those roses on her cheeks,
mother said, meant T.B.

But it would be all right
when Frances came.

And those fungi
camping in corners
and the case of the dead bat
in the meat safe
yes it would be all right
when Frances came.

Mother said, we must impress Frances,
clean up the kitchen, make all ship shape,
so I dressed up like All Hallows Eve
and Frances came.

She came and swept through
the house like Dracula,
she raped us, drew blood
satin red and smooth.
She was a volcano
and lava ran unstinted
over furnishings and beds
and carpets squirmed and floundered

as if the Lough Ness monster
lurked beneath them.

She scoured the buildings,
the barn, the cowshed,
she ravished the grass
between the cobbles in the yard
like she was shaving an old man's
chin for the sacrament.

I hid. I hid in the grease
of the chestnut tree. I hid
in the elbow of the laurel.
I hid in the maw of the bran
barrel. I put on my lemon dress
and lay in a field of buttercups
and Frances came.

I gathered strength
and turned my art to the darkened well
over the hill of Confey.
I scooped and scraped off the viscous scum
where all life teemed in miniature.
I built a temple under the lichened stone
like a father's purse where all wealth
teems in miniature
and Frances came.

Mother said it would be all right
when Frances settled down.

Although she cooked like
a German General, attacked
the bright red lumps of meat
as if they were Jews, Mother said

it would be all right
when Frances settled down.

I cradled my terror,
hid my obstinacy
and Mother screamed: Lunacy,
Frances is a jewel.

I had to agree at night
when God came down and kicked
the chamber pot at the foot of my bed.
I had to kneel and pray
for yeast that would rise my soul
like Christmas cake,
but my soul went off like kettle steam.
I tried to call it back.
It was Aladdin: new souls for old
and Frances came.

It's the fever, she said
as she sat like dough
on the foot of my bed.
You see, mother said,
it's all right now.
When the fever went I could rise
from bed, provided I dressed up warm
and avoided draughts.

I tramped the house,
like a tiddly-wink I jumped
from squares into pots.
I was my best toy dog
and straw came out of my chest.
I was Minnie Mouse in Mother's
high-heeled shoes.
But Frances owned my soul.

In safe keeping, she said,
and her iceberg head
jerked widely and wisdom
snorted through her nose.

Now I must pray to Frances,
go on my knees at night
because Frances held my soul
between her fists like a rubber ball.

But one day
one duck egg-coloured day
Frances leaned out of the window,
she leaned out and spoke
to the air like a racial memory.

I stood in all this speaking,
silent behind Frances,
I basked in this and I was
secret as a wasp crawling into the jam.

Frances was now lady-God,
lady-God resting, and I was
lady-God's toy into which
she could replace my soul
like a key into a walking doll.

But I was unwound and rubber,
If she turned round and put her hand
on my stomach I'd say "Ma ma".

But I knew there was more to God
than just Frances. There must be proof
right inside Frances. So I crept nearer.
I was moonsilence, I was Rumpelstiltskin

hiding my name
and I was unguessable. I lifted
up Frances' skirt
and flung it over her head.

You will soon be a big girl,
Mother said, and there are things
you'll learn about then.

I won't beat you limp
like a rabbit-skin, but what a pity
now that everything was so ship-shape
that Frances had to leave.

I swallowed my soul
and it went down like a raw potato.
When Mother had seen to this
she told me that there was a girl
in the village called Myra.
Pity she's an R.C., Mother said,
but it would be all right
when Myra came.

Outside *The Odeon,* Camden Town

The snow on the street like stewed apple
the buses slopslopping past
with carton-loads of Paddies.
In the illuminated cheek-bones
of the Odeon cinema
on my twenty-ninth birthday I waited.

An aeroplane took off in Arizona
and Buddy Holly died.

Last week Elvis Presley
felt his chest grip the skin – felt
his shrivelled parts like an empty money belt
quiver for the last time.

I am not weeping for an old star's death
or a man stumbling in secrecy
to an appointment with a mediocre end
but myself gone forty-nine with memories
of my first record player and a bunch
of 45s and a Greek boy
separating air from vowels:

"Will you come … ba-by… will you come?"

Before Going Up

Before going up
she downed a pint of cooking sherry.

How was it, she asked afterwards.

Good, he said, for you?

Fine.

First

A dog should die outside, the others said,
but I had taken her
scrunched up in my arms,
hidden her in the shed.

We lay together in a shroud of hay
holding death aside
like the curtain in a theatre.
But then it came: the blood.
It spurted from her mouth,
spurted on the flagstones
like a string of beads.

What follows obliterates,
with each new loss,
that accident of grief.
But how can one forget what was one's
first. First anything, first love,
first loss, first kiss.

Crybaby

for John McLachlan

Her neighbours talked
with wasps in their teeth:
We heard your baby crying,
crying half the night.

Sweet chain of love, she shouted
that binds me to my child.

(She was at a party down the road
the night the host hanged himself.)

Snow Love

Dublin is not accustomed
to this thick white coat.
It has crept back into silence
in a cemetery of time.

With the crack of the clock
the traffic starts; slow splashing
wheels make newly furrowed lines
filthy beneath this creaking skin
while day hangs up the sun
like a plug of orange tobacco.

We are happy to be ritually forgotten,
lucky to belong to this great
redundant mass on this cold day.
To be free to count each others' bones
beneath the bedclothes.

That wheeling spectacle beyond the glass
has all our sympathy, by God!
But we are free to make – repeat –
a blessing of each bone

Till the short day melts
like a candle in its saucer
and snow peters down once more
like silent falling stars.

How My True Love and I Lay Without Touching

How my true love and I lay without touching
How my hand journeyed to the drumlin of his hip
my pelvis aching
Just like two saints or priests or nuns
my true love and I lay without touching.

How I would long for the brush of a kiss
to travel my cheek or the cheek of my groin
my heart aching
But just like two saints or priests or nuns
my true love and I lay without touching.

Last night in my dreams I spoke with his wife
his true love who had left him surely as they lay
    without touching
my heart for her was aching
For like two saints or priests or nuns
the two loves once lay without touching,

But the dream of her faded before concentrating
each to each in our innocent mutual hating
her hand aching
to blind me with bullets to prevent herself from pining
for a once-love she longed for and lay without touching.

Now my true love lies in the mutton of madness.
"I was always troubled by sex," he says, with great sadness,
his wife and I aching
in our cold single beds with many seas dividing
as we think of the years we spent without touching.

From a Painting by Artemesia Gentileschi

How strange to be wielding this knife
with such violence.
Regard the bounce of muscle on my arm,s
between my fingers the scarlet beads
of victory.

Who is beneath my bloodied hand
(if they name me wanton then I am
as is he between my nimble fingers).
But for convenience I have named him Holofernes
and she? The woman hacking off his head?
I call her Judith (how pretty in comparison
her hand maid – assistant in this direful deed.
Great gentle hands – the midwife
hovering over the labour bed.)

I do not pierce my breast with thorns,
the red rose has no song for me.
(Rose–white my bosom – pure –
clean as foam on the crest of a wave.
I cleanse my palette with this violent act.)
Later I shall paint the humble, the heroic.

Chain Strokes

The breathing began at eight p.m.
Two starched nurses – angry swans –
In my head the sonata – B-flat minor –
That was my sleep,
Restless chromatic quavers.

I awoke.
Lento. Again *lento.*

She died at eight a.m.
Ten years later
I read *Sons and Lovers.*

Exiles

for Geraldine O'Reilly

Those were the seedlings we sowed
pricked and primed against the hard
rocks of poverty.

Those were the seedlings –
we have put names on their
children. The children
of Gurlay Flynn and Mother Jones –
Oh your America

Tumbletown and Dead River Valley.
Famine-forced they crowded the canals
from the bog of Allen to Idaho.
Crossed the Atlantic
in the stench of homelessness.

Now Bridie, don't forget to say your prayers.

Mother, get me a bride
from out the four green fields –
my fields.

Mean fields.

Some hid behind the lace
others shed stone tears
Useless tears.

To hell with the bleeding fingers
of all the women
(A nickel a day, make hay make hay)

Cooking fat at night
in the quiver of the candle.

We'll show you who the boss is,
you Irish bitches.

*Now Bridie, keep your legs crossed
and the rosary between your toes.*

But they rose ... rose
like bonfires on a mountain,
every mansheila of them
rose against the whips,
broke files, made unions.
It was a slow going –
a slow coming.

*Dear Bridie, I received the dollars.
Your father's taken ill,
I got shoes for Peadar
and Kathleen.
I'll put the rest by.
Pray for me.*

Why are we waiting?
Give me the DC9
New York, New World,
New suitcase, transit visa.

*Uncle Tom, find me a husband
and a Green Card
and I'll never leave
your America.
My Green Card.*

Mean Card.

This is your pilot,
pointing pilot,
feathering down on Kennedy Airport
Oh America!

I strike out now
in a skyscrape of desire
quivering for dollars.
You mean I've come all the way from Clontarf
and there's no job?

Why is everyone sleeping
in the subway?

These are the seedlings we sow
pricked and primed against
the hard rocks of poverty.

We put names on these children
the children of Gurlay Flynn
and Mother Jones.

Oh your America.

Remembering the Blindness of Jorge Luis Borges

He went off last year
To – I hope – some far-seeing place.
At that fearsome Taoiseach do
I took his quilted hand
barely murmuring how honoured
I was to meet him
With Byronic irony he muttered,
So is everyone else.

De donde viene este vino?
In that dark world
we were invisible accomplices
bandits without a cause
banderilleros without a bull.

Penumbra – shadow – poet of eternal light.

Breach Baby

Black panther, he does not
streak through forests.
Back and forth, back and forth
in this house of his.
In this house of his, he paces.

My son who is gone five –
the solitary watcher –
says quietly:

He does not know which way.

He remembers my rib-cage.

Pointless

You go on and on.

But imagine the world without music.
Just imagine – no fifths, no thirds,
no arpeggios, no atonal notes.
(And surely God invented the octave.)

I once saw a horse dance in Phoenix Park.

Yes you go on and on
saying art, unless political, is pointless.
But you don't pick blackberries with me,
you are not interested in mud.

Clondalkin Concrete

Late again! You know we keep regular hours
in Clondalkin Concrete.

I was the Temp.
The one who worked from five-past-nine till six
with no let-up.
But they kept regular hours at Clondalkin Concrete.

From Clondalkin Concrete I wrote a letter to Paul.
I told him I was writing concrete verse
and very soon I would send them, block on block.
In Clondalkin Concrete we keep stanzas
numbered and counted carefully, cement and sand.
We keep regular poems in Clondalkin Concrete.

All the while I worked in Clondalkin Concrete
I must have sold a million tons of blocks.
I was a bungalow blitz of a typist,
invoice-neat in my work.
But I wrote, Dear Paul, I dedicate to you
every block of a concrete stanza,
every freezing grain of sand,
for I'm up to my neck in Clondalkin Concrete.

While directly gazing into my boss's watery studs,
All that Fall, I shouted, All that Fall.

Moth Dust

Pumpkin fond pumpkin
had water under the chin,
it didn't matter.
It didn't matter then, until
his eyes became two asterisks,
his back a scythe,
and with his dainty fingers
he filled my mouth with sloes,
my mind with moth dust.

But he left Mohammed's thumbprint
on my shoulder.

Children's Games

for William and Anna Bardwell

Once upon a time
I saw my two children playing
where Karl Marx was lying
with a tombstone on his head;
they were naked from the waist down

and the English around and around said
Better the children dead
than naked from the waist down

Now I was a foreigner
on that cold Highgate Hill
but I bore no ill to the English
no ill

So I toiled away by the Spaniards
where the English were all lovers
and their legs gleamed O
so cold and naked
naked from the waist down

And I tried another graveyard
and found another plot
where Sigmund Freud was lying
in his eiderdown of weeds

My children, I said, romp away
this little strip is yours
for the dead are mostly idle
and do not care if you are naked
naked from the waist down

and the graves began to smile
and the hymn of England fade
and my children took out their pocket knives
and carved on the limey stone:

Dr Freud lies here in the nettles
we are dancing on his head

Her Sister's Child

Her sister's child is sleeping with her husband
and she is not a bit surprised.
He loved her far too much to stake his all,
(he said); she's not so sure,
the baby leaves his bed at five.

Her sister's child is blonde and bonnie and blithe,
at twenty-one a little immature
(perhaps a little indiscreet?),
should be more circumspect, you'd think.

>   When she is far away
>   and still alive she'll tell
>   this story with more subtlety.

After Pushkin

A pinch of laughter opened up his face
"Irish?" he said. "Ireland!"
"What do you do there really?"
With O a wave of nonchalance, "You know," I said –
Write poems, books, you know, that sort of thing –
Waste a lot of trees …"

A ring of comprehension. "Rabbie Burns," he said.
"Ah no, that other lot – O'Casey, Joyce –
A different kettle of Celtic fish."

"I see," he said, his tiny specs
transparent flowers of recognition.
"*The Portrait,* him I know, I like him much –
I just stamp passports."

I had stepped across his threshold
from this pin in the Atlantic
and placed my brief amongst the idols
and the pictures – Akhmatova, Osip and Nadezda –
The Rubens, Caravaggios, Matisses.
All histories combine – and he
who takes no part in this idiot
warp and woof of words
gazes at me sternly from his window,
nodding, sees how turning in a circle
everything comes round.

Memory

I remember my mother who hated onions,
sex and mongrel dogs,
my father's rusty fingers
wading through butterflies.
So I grew to talk kindly with enemies,
soldiers and policemen.
I stare into the morphine of memory,
pressing the needle into the weakest spot.

I wonder does she hold her skirt around her knees
in the heaven she believed in,
the demon sex beaten to a dish-cloth
with semi-colons of *thou shalt nots*,
full stops of self abasement,
or does she lie, legs splayed out
for dogs and pictures and others to enter her
face glazed in anticipation
for something she never experienced before.

Last week I visited her grave.
A dead wreath had landed askew the weathered cross.
Good day, Ma, I said and lifted the crumbling crown
and hurled it into the fields of Confey.

On Mistaking a Jesuit Lecture for a Poetry Reading

"Is this the poetry reading?"
Shh ... all heads turn in my direction.
I settle down beside a balding man
and listen to the speaker.
He tells of Paris, nineteen eighty-eight,
of how the doors are open every day.
I wait to hear how poets have been entertained
and housed and watered freely
but not a word of verse or stanza,
crutch or limp is coming from his lips.
This is a long long intro, think I,
looking at the man whose rim of hair
is tonsure-like
(but surely tonsures have gone out, think I).
He sneers unfriendlily, I draw my breath
uncross my knees, look round for the three poets
I came to hear. No poet. No familiar face,
and then the awful truth!
I am the only woman in the place.
"Ahem," I mutter through my tonsils,
"Where do you think I am?"
A howl of *shhishes* echoes from the ashtray walls
Mr Tonsure very nearly spits.
Now my buttocks are experiencing the sting
of tensing muscles – my knee has gone to sleep,
I dare not move. I feel like shouting "Fire!"
or anything that might get me out
but everything's against me, doors are closed,
no doubt I am locked in. Perhaps I'm dead
and this is where the wretched sinners
go – to poetry readings in the sky

where smoking is forbidden
and Jesuits interminably drool
about the good that they have done below,
and no poet sings.

Lion

Grandpa paced the avenue,
tired old lion –
forwards, turn and back
as though with every step
his luggage lightened
as though the years
were falling back
to the hide-and-seek
of childhood.

He said he'd die on Wednesday.
On Tuesday, a wintry night,
clouds buffeting, no moon,
he took his final walk.
He stopped just once
to pat his pockets,
to reassure himself
he'd jetissoned the dross,
shook out his chalk-white mane
and climbed the stairs.

At the funeral my grandma said,
"He was a meticulous gentleman."

Dostoevsky's Grave

I am locked in this acropolis
just Feodor and me
I rub my fingers
in his overcoat of stone
gambling my airline ticket
and find in the valley
of my life-line
the gravel of Baden Baden

In Memoriam John Jordan

We were long on the one bitch road
Between the 'Hatch' and that 'Low' Leeson Street
Haring through Agatha Christies (you)
Or on some parched afternoon
We'd bump into a waiting moment
With a *how d'you do how are you*
(As Eddie Maguire used to say)
Or your apocryphal pronouncement
"May God forgive me, all my enemies
Down at one go."

In Grogan's bar with mongering dole-men
Adroop or clattering drunk
The silent country of your endurance
Was something that stepped aside
However insecure the footing
Uninviting the ravines
Conversing with that other John
A Chaplinesque half-sided smile
An *Oh dear me,* to save a fall or two.

After the fireworks have subsided
We will sing old songs
La recherche du temps perdu
And birds will call as though insensed.

Dawn Guest

My patch of lawn between poplar and oak
Is empty once again. For a moment
In an agony of pride he raised his antlers,
Whipped the wind, leapt and was gone.

Perhaps he was never there
Between oak and poplar
This dawn visitor. Too much beauty
Destroys the levels of concentration.

But ever since I've watched this patch of grass
As if he still was there – sinews locked for flight
As though we could in one split second
Give skin for skin, muscle for rippling muscle.

Still he lives on in my mind's eye,
What I've invested in him
Like an episode of tremendous luck,
The pot of gold at the end of the rainbow.

Brother

If only he would admit to being born
my brother. Every Christmas, without fail,
a cheque arrives – the nervous cutting of the knife –
it goes up yearly with inflation.
Hastily I post my New Year card – the feast is over –
clip off another piece of guilt
like breaking off an edge of biscuit.

I know that he'll outlive me,
this wombless man. He'll pay
the undertaker, scowl mysteriously
at my friends – a motley crew.
Later he'll read my obituary in the press
and find out things he never knew.

History Stopped That Night

It might have been anyone
but the fact that it was I
who lay in a mulch of leaves
between two ice ages
watching your face in shadow
speckled like seed-cakes
in a bronze moon-madness, harvest for size,
made me wonder at luck that
makes a twist of time
so unimportant. Morning, I woke
a shelf of moss had curled itself into a pillow,
it was damp and cold. And you slept deep, I think.

History had undone itself like buttons on a coat.
We had played farms and families for centuries
of weeping land, gone off, made good or bad,
adopted transatlantic ways and accents,
become colonial, racist, over sentimental,
the hovel of our past made glorious
in the quick-buck game and fuck the wogs.

My duty then was to make sure
that he who lay beside me woke that day
though mulch and hypnum might invade
our nostrils all too soon
beneath the forest-floor of someone else's sorrow.

But coming from the hostelry that night
we'd kissed each other flat
and mottled by moon light
fallen like Icarus in history's flight.

Letter to my Teacher

I am speeding the Esker townland
on my fairy cycle.
I am seven and the day is grained
with a fine Kildare mist.
It is moist as a bull's nose.
I drive my face into it as into a wash-tub,
my neck cools. At the edge of the golf course
a lorry passes; mud cakes like chocolate
on my socks.

They have thrown me out for writing poems.
Now I am telling you this before I die
I am telling you this in a letter.
Poems were bad, they said,
so from seven on I knew.
Iris Wellwood you were my teacher,
Iris Wellwood of the sun-red hair,
come all the way from Cavan town
to throw me out for writing poems.

Now I've been thrown out from everywhere,
pubs, houses, public transport,
and the only reason far's I know
is that frogs keep jumping off the paper,
mosquitoes dancing in the cubic yard of my skull
from Leeson Street to Kopovar
from Leningrad on the Nevsky Prospekt
to Clanbrassil Street on the Villamos.

You taught me seven nines were sixty-three
but writing poems was a waste of time.
I write this letter with sincerest thanks

now that nine times seven years
are nearly gone. I've ridden that fairy bike
a long long way from Esker, Confey or Spion Kop
through the earliest townlands of my mind,
the townlands of Muslin and Esther Waters.

Note

for Jacqueline Bardwell

The trouble is I miss the short sea
in an alcove of rock or the wider
more impelling stretch of the Atlantic.
I seem to be paralysed between two Drumlins
and the trees against the pewter clouds
unnerve me as though to say "I know your number".

Still at the moment, all is well
and when the time is right
I shall go – there are other places
somewhere with a Russian wind talking down the chimney
and the Black Sea breaking wilfully
beyond the reaches of Chekov's garden.

CT Scan

They've put my head inside the big machine.
Jack the cat stalks round my brain.
He purrs, he kneads,
his paws are soft as mushrooms.
He has triumphant eyes.

They talk casually
on the intercom
about stomach pills and airline sickness.

I lie still as stone in this aluminium trunk
thinking of Mary Shelley.

A Single Rose

I have willed my body to the furthering of science.
Although I'll not be there
to chronicle my findings
I can imagine all the students
poring over me:
"My God, is that a liver?
And those brown cauliflowers are lungs?"
"Yes, sir, a fine example of how not to live."
"And what about the brain?"
"Alas the brain. I doubt if this poor sample
ever had one." As with his forceps
he extracts a single rose.

Roses

My aunt Joyce had the roses
roses of consumption
two round rose buds
blood-red roses
roses of consumption
on her cheeks.

In the teeming Mayo rain
every year in the hired house
was when we heard the sea say "Joyce".
We children heard it – "Joyce" –
while the waves dragged back the stones
with a terrifying "oh".

We'd offer her the silence of the mirror
a powder puff, a comb,
and bundled in all kinds of coats
we'd carry her
to Ballycastle, Glenamoy, Belderg or Bunnahowen,
anywhere the sea would growl her name
and she could sit and listen quietly.

But they were cleverer than we
with pills and pillows; in the end a wooden box,
they laid her in it like you would a bunch of flowers
in a shoe box – roses maybe,
and then we heard the thump of roses,
earth and roses – roses
like the blood-red roses on her cheeks.

The Price of Shoes in Russia

I am an old old woman, *Izvinite*.
My fingers are nicotine brown
from endless fags. But I exult
in the wings of the choir
that swing from within
the walls of the cathedral.

Till another old old woman,
older even than I, jumps on me
with the speed of hate,
cleaves my head with her umbrella
and calls her grandson to evict me.

Being no fool in my eightieth year
I stuff the burning orb into my pocket.
Izvinite, I am old and stupid as a dog.
I beg forgiveness on my hands and knees.
He tells me his name is Yuri.

Yes I'm Yuri – Yuri from Kharkov.
And I'm an ancient Protestant woman
from a Catholic country called Ireland
and I wish I'd never smoked
in the precincts of his church.
Oh Yuri, I cry. But Yuri does not beat me.
He sits me down in the mellow shadow of a tree
near the puddled fish pond in the park
and talks of shoes.

Shoes, he says, lighting up,
are very dear in Kharkov.
I take his *Cosmos* gratefully, inhale and cry.
Oh yes, but they are also dear in Dublin,
Shoes in Dublin are exceptionally dear.

But socks, he cries, we queue for socks,
Not to mention stockings, I say.

He is shaken with a fine delight
as we work our way up thighwards
and I burn slowly – from inside with a scorching love,
from my pocket from the burning cigarette,
and from the sun above my double-vented skull.

When we embrace we agree to meet in Yalta
and feed cyclamen seeds through the eyelids
of Chekov's dacha.

The Bingo Bus

In Killinarden there was nothing –
Nothing – but nearer town
There was the Bingo Bus,

The Bingo Bus, the Bingo Bus,
Nearer to Thee, my God, the Bingo Bus,
And *Strip the Willow* they played
With the driver, trussed the conductor –
Danced *Turkey in the Straw.*

Every Thursday without fail
The ladies rode on the Bingo Bus,

And Booze before Bingo and after
And lots of Booze in between,
Returning late from Bingo
They ate the conductor whole.

We in Killinarden wanted O so much
To have a Bingo Bus of our own.

We wrote to the Authorities,
Begged and begged on our knees.
TDs were hammered, we marched,
Made flags, went on hunger strike
Outside the Dail.

You lot aren't ready for Bingo,
You've only been here a year,
You must have lots more babies
Before you deserve a Bingo Bus.

So every year to the clinic,
Three out, one in, four out, one in,
But still no Bingo Bus.

I had to leave Killinarden
Wearied from making flags,
Marching and lobbying and having kids.
So I moved right into a hotel.
St. Brendan's is its name.

I make sanitary towels for Bingo players,
I do my bit for Bingo players,
I am on the ball for Bingo players,
I'm saving up for Bingo,
Saving up for Bingo.

Lila's Potatoes

They asked me to write a poem
about Lila's potatoes.
I thought about the eighteen-forties,
I thought about watercress,
I thought about weeds,
but they were black,
my plants were black.
Lazy beds, they said, were OK.

I had spent my life in lazy beds
one way and another – lazy beds
in and out of lazy beds.

They'd got me every where
when I slept in different towns,
places, seas – another child,
lazy beds, they said, were OK, in the famine.

I saw my plants – black – leaves black
stalks black – lazy beds, they said –
in the famine – lazy beds.

So I made kids in lazy beds – strapping women
all from lazy beds – eight altogether
they got jobs in underground London pubs,
strip halls – make-believe – run around
and ended up in lazy beds all eight of them.

Lazy beds make black potatoes – Lila's potatoes
have the blight – lazy beds – Lila's potatoes
they got the blight.
Then Seamus took the bad luck out of it.

It was the sun, he said, caused it.
I often wondered what caused all my children.
I'm glad it was the sun.

Them's Your Mammy's Pills

for Edward McLachlan

They'd scraped the top soil off the garden
and every step or two they'd hurled a concrete block
bolsters of mud like hippos from the hills
rolled on the planters plantings of the riff-raff of the city.

The schizophrenic planners had finished off their job
folded their papers, put away their pens –
the city clearances were well ahead.

And all day long a single child was crying
while his father shouted: Don't touch them,
them's your mammy's pills.

I set to work with zeal to play 'Doll's House',
'Doll's Life', 'Doll's Garden'
while my adolescent sons played 'Temporary Heat'
in the living room out front
and drowned the opera of admonitions:
Don't touch them, them's your mammy's pills.

Fragile as needles the women wander forth
laddered with kids, the unborn one ahead
to forge the mile through mud and rut
where mulish earth-removers rest, a crazy sculpture.

They are going back to the city for the day
this is all they live for –
going back to the city for the day.

The line of shops and solitary pub
are camouflaged like check points on the border

the supermarket stretches emptily
a circus of sausages and time
the till-girl gossips in the veg department
Once in a while a woman might come in
to put another pound on
the electronic toy for Christmas.

From behind the curtains every night
the video lights are flickering, butcher blue
Don't touch them, them's your mammy's pills.

No one has a job in Killinarden
nowadays they say it is a no-go area
I wonder, then, who goes and does not go
in this strange forgotten world
of video and valium.

I visited my one time neighbour
not so long ago. She was sitting
in the hangover position.
I knew she didn't want to see me
although she'd cried when we were leaving.

I went my way
through the quietly rusting motor cars and prams,
past the barricades of wire, the harmony of junk.
The babies that I knew are punk-size now
and soon children will have children
and new voices ring the *leit motif:*

Don't touch them, them's your mammy's pills.

An Unusual Irish Summer

for Nicholas McLachlan

I ask them have they brought the galleys.
I am alive and awake with a hole in my head.
My son's face swings above me
like an extraordinary coin.
I'd been dreaming of water chestnuts
and the heat beneath my skull
makes me long for that apron of sand
stretching out to the country's eye
in an unusual Irish summer.

Kassia

Kassia, the 9th century Byzantine poet,
wore epigrams like bangles on her arms;
when offered marriage with the emperor
she scalded him with wit.

Banished from the court,
Columns of stone will kneel,
she said, *before you change a fool.*

A learned fool, God save us.
The pigs are eating pearls.

Skipping Banville in Barcelona

for Colm Tóibín

I am infinitely caused
beneath the pinnacles of Gaudi.
Mesmerising struts, angels,
apostles, dog-lion,
timber and stone.
"There are no straight lines
in nature," Gaudi said.

The quilted edifice towers
twin pinnacles (God can only
see downwards), religious
phalluses – bourgeois trinkets,
gingerbread and wine.

Retiring afterwards to remember
and cool down, I pick up *The Book of Evidence*,
watch Carmen being murdered once again,
remember previous jealousies and loves,
and spend the evening
skipping Banville in Barcelona.

Maggie's Cottage

for Geraldine Whelan

There we kept time pressed apart
like a row of books supported by two book-ends,
there we erased the pitch and toss
of all the lives we'd lived –
the potholes of disaster.

The "where oh where" of now is the question of that time
when as Vladimir and Estragon we walked the avenue
with our water bottles of laughter, our occasional fights.
We flew saucers of friendship above the stars
which landed in the lap of the 'Big House'
as when dawn brought the demon Harding to cook our
breakfast complete with pike and hangover.

If the snake of time has shed its skin again
I know that artichokes are different from thistles.
We left our marks – a painted room – a broken pane of glass,
a hedge of beans, a colony of spinach.

The Noise of Masonry Settling

The Knowledge of Beezie McGowan

She knows where the whelks gather,
The booty of waves,
The mussels.

She knows where the limpets lie,
How the rocks
Are spreading.

She knows where the dilisk hides
In the pitted cracks
When the water's ebbing.

She can tell the storm
By the heron's flight
From cliff to harbour,

But wages were poor
In this industry of God's,
The learning got, so hard, so hard.

Moving House

The house unfolds and straightens with relief.
We've discarded the stone, the elephant,
the Japanese parasol and the pile
of unfinished poems.
They are like rotten fruit,
might be a core worth extracting.

Are you taking the piano? Yes.
The mice are nesting in the keys
And sit with paws crossed like expectant choirboys.

We are tired of this move
And all the other moves we've made,
And tired of the people who are tired
Of carting memories around.

The magic of summer took us by the neck
And wrung us out like an old sock.
Is it possible we've accumulated
So much rubbish in so short a time?

Let us go then quickly before dark.
In this way we'll close the shutters of absence
And find a new set of attachments and trivia.

'These Aspirins Seem To Be No Use'
Last Words of Ernest Shakleton,
Died of Angina Pectoris, January 4th, 1922

for my cousin Robbie

What possessed you
On that last trip, sucking on the fags,
Drinking champagne by the neck,
Imagining your poor heart
Could get you there and back?

As your heart couldn't follow,
You followed it
Like all great explorers –
Emily Brontë, saying
'You can send for the doctor now,'
Tolstoy, doing press-ups
at the railway station,
Flaubert wishing
He hadn't written *Madame Bovary* ...

Maybe it's the pure whiteness
The spirit needs
That drives one on in the end.

I'll Do the Messages

I'll do the messages,
Give me the poison drops
From the orphan's tongue.
I'll pre-digest the wrong.

I'll sell the flags for the flag-seller
And hold the tiresome horse
For the smith with four dead wives.

The apple is in your side, my brother.
I'll learn the Blue Danube
From the village dressmaker.
I am the scape-goat and I'll dance
To someone else's tune.

Ten tall sunflowers grew in my garden.
They played the incomparable artist's game:
One black eye each and a dart
That was the start of my garden.

I walked through the trees of adolescence,
The angry walnut and sheltering beech.
A seed was sown in an ebony heart.
Let the bud decide where the flower shall fall.

Hard to Imagine Your Face Dead

Hard to imagine your face dead,
Not giving out, pontificating,
Just quiet, serene, the moustache resting
Over the broken tooth.

Those eyes – no longer
Like water brimming
Over a gutter caught with sun.

Your shoulders, no longer alert
In your cushion of death,
Their anger subsiding.

Better to imagine you lying
Alone and listless,
Like when the speed used to leave you
In the downbeat of your madness.

For Dermot and Anne Marie
on Attending the Birth of Dallan

Pimlico and Vauxhall Bridge
And that sally-port near the Tate
Where barges lie deck to deck
Like lesbians, and Blake
Has burnt Satan in Milton's house.

Tantalus up to his waist
In the Thames can't drink,
Though the water leans on his thighs.
Pimlico and Eleanor Rigby
At the end of the Chelsea game.

Pimlico and splinter city
Jostle for life under cranes.
'Bow down to the artists,
Those birds have no wings, boy,
They sing for their supper.'

Pimlico and Adam's rib
Have put their names on the list.
The morainic wastes are groaning
At the end of the map,
But the compass is spinning.

In Pimlico live Harlequin
And cat – look fast for the
Shadows they leave. Citizens stir
In their sleep, and Hesperus
Sneaks shrough the grimy window.

In Pimlico the lending library
Lies on the hem of Cat's hair
On the pillow; the hazel strand
Is the margin of waiting allowed,
Like the whiskey dream of slow water spreading.

Where the Grass is Dark with Trees

for Dan

I want to walk in the field
Where the grass is dark with trees

I want to take the hand of the past
As round and clean as an autumn apple

And hold it tight as a nail
Till all the talking is done

For the seabird's cry is still the saddest

Lobster Fishing

Lend me your education,
Glum Clare man,
While your sockless boots
Slide on the algae

Under the jawbone of cliff,
Whipped by the anxious sleeves of wind.
The night air burns with salt.
The cliffs shout back at the sea,
Their gun-metal mouths
Hungry for lacey kisses.

We have eased ourselves down,
Promoted the cliff-stairs to safe passage
Above the sea-howl, each step
Widening on to the outcrop of armoured rock
Making its individual sound as the sea-plants crack,
'Beach the bloody crates!'

Orders is orders
For he is no crazy man: pots are expensive,
A living must be got.
His anger swings in the storm like a metal moon.
No caution allowed
In these recondite surroundings.

It was fighting for hours, it seemed,
The wet ropes rasping already frozen fingers
Till crowding back on the baize shelves of Kilbaha
The crates are counted. Six. All safe.
He is exultant. The ocean swell behind us
We'll go to Kilrush and later cash the cheque.

Yet for me, when the thin line of dawn
Splinters the kitchen window,
I am concious of a poor green thing
Too small to sell and ready for the pot.

I should much prefer to tie it on a string
And prance upon a street
Mindful of Gerard de Nerval.

Oh Well! *(de mortuis ... etc)*

Climbing the spinal steps,
The vertebraic ladder,
The fieldmouse of panic
Creeps silently

In the heel of night,
The skin of her anger
Racing from terminal to terminal,
Dodging and doubling back
From the campanology
Of the mortuary doors.

Gráinne dragging fishtails
To the mountain cave.

The West's Asleep

Death comes handy, they say,
When the leaf snaps,
Sleeps and stalks back,
When the bud quickens.
Two months that bring up the toll.

As the years pass
The houses empty.
No light shines from the windows,
No dogs bark on the long road
That hangs from Cloonagh.

A straggling beard
Of ragweed, thistle, goosefoot,
And the wild cup of the rose
Calls out the names:
Tom, The Black Doctor,
Ellie, Sarah, Jack.
Ah sure,
They're all gone now
And none to come after.

That Day

Either
Daryl V. Zanuch or
Cecil B. DeMille
Said, *I employed*
Gary Cooper
The day
He got old.

Can ordinary people,
Who are not
Film directors
Recognise that day
Without being told?

Office Vignette

Mr. Blank sat on his office stool
Dictating to Miss Brazen
The beauties of profit.
'Screw me,' she said,
When she came to the billion pound paragraph.
He did, on the edge-to-edge.
Unscrewed, she resumed her task.
Miss Flower, on the other hand,
The artistic type, couldn't bear it.
So much pink flesh on the carpet,
So much force against the waste-paper basket,
So much paper on the floor,
And all because of
The high interest rate regime
In the corollary of a falling currency.
Mr. Blank sat on his office stool
Looking at Miss Flower.
He was expecting rain.

My Brother Reggie

My brother Reggie
Was generous with epithets –
Face-ache, Vim Tin, Toast-rack –
Not without a trace
Of humour. Why not let
Me be Maid of the Track?
I asked. It did not
Crack his face.

My brother Reggie
Liked to put the pillow
Over my head, and press,
Press down so
Till my head was flat.
He said, *I want you dead.*
But what fun is there in that?

My Brother Reggie,
A gentleman to his guts,
Is a hundred years old
And hedges his bets.
He doesn't care to put
His hands round my throat
And squeeze me weird.
Like a goat,
He just hugs his beard.

Love Poem

The nicest thing
You ever said to me
Was
Do we always have to live
Like Bonnie and Clyde?

The Night's Empty Shells

I am always afraid
They will find me
Like the skinned arm of the child,

Break the joint between
The ulna and the radius,
Gouge out the mephitic matter,

Take the dance from my feet,
Splay the small bones,
Work the cement into the instep
Before I have settled the measure.

I am not here to ogle the sea,
Count the brent geese,
On the short strand below Ardtrasna,

I'm here to learn the light of Lislarry
Where shone the shebeen once:
A fisherman's star.

So sailed Praeger
After breakfast of poitín
And cold potatoes – a note

To the waves – a leaky boat,
A nod to the dawn
On the East of Innismurray.

For once on my gable
A beacon shone,
The end of the sea lane

To a safe hauling
Of the night's empty shells.

Heart Trouble

It was the heart, after all,
That let her down.
So she lay under the frown
Of the cardiologist,
Thinking:
At least this is respectable.
It might have been me found
Dead drunk in someone else's kitchen.

Innismurray

> *'Where there's a cow there's a woman and where there's a woman, there's mischief'*
> — *St Colmcille, who founded the monastery and banned all cows from the island*

Two thumb holes in the birthing stone
Beside the women's graveyard.

There she squats, prayers
Breaking from parched lips

To the great Man-God to deliver her
From the yearly gall of labour,

To beg for a man-child
To erase the guilt of her sex.

For being a woman
Has no pardon,

Skirts raised in the wind
On an island that floats

Like a bayleaf
In the unforgiving sea.

She crouches thus
Till the infant lies in the scutch

And she looks at the unmarked grave
Beneath whose soil her mother lies.

She ponders.

We Don't Serve Travelling People

The barman attacks the counter,
His dry cloth bolting in fury
Along the plastic beam.
His eyes like electric studs
Fasten on to me.

I feel the familiar pain.

We don't serve travelling people
Or prostitutes.

No, I am not popular in pubs.
Nine out of ten times I hear
That icy 'madam' cast upon the shore
Of my uncomplaining retreat.

Not here not there – from Liffey Street
To Donnybrook and back –
There's nowhere left, it seems,
To rest the prostitution
Of my weary but travelling mind.

'No Road Beyond the Graveyard'

— Chief Inspector Morse in a novel by Colin Dexter

But the No Road beyond the graveyard
Is full of possibilities,
Eidetic visions, ghosts,
The valedictory sigh, perhaps.
But when I stand on this No Road,
I am thinking of an old woman
Who took the shoes of her son
And polished them, polished them,
Till you could see your face in them,
First the left, then the right,
And placed them under the kitchen table
Before she died. And the son
Stands at the No Road
In the dulled shoes,
In a hopeless frame of mind.
There's no reason for this No Road.
No mention of falling stones,
Dangerous cliffs
Likely to flood.
Simply No Road,
No five-barred gate,
No 'Dogs Keep Out',
No 'Danger Men at Work',
No 'Closed for Repair',
Just, beyond the graveyard,
'No Road'.
No cul de sac, no boreen
No bridle path.
The road doesn't go nowhere,
It simply isn't.

It's quiet too in the graveyard
No creature, no bird,
No field mouse. Quiet.
Rows upon rows of stones
Crosses, inscriptions, dates,
But quiet. In the end
One keeps one's ghosts
To oneself.

Hawthornden Castle

These forces on the battlements
Make snakes pass through her bloodstream.
Lecherous ghosts torment her
With the hooting
Of the distant owl. She cannot sleep
On this moonlit plain
To the ticking of the Rosewell mine,
The town ill-named with its stumpy streets,
Mean houses pasted over
With a coal-dust sheen.
She remembers, too, the hedgehog,
Lifeless, lying
Like a discarded gardener's glove.

Drum Up a Poem

Drum up a poem,
They said, *for Eddie's birthday,*
And me as empty as
An upturned barrel.

Who then is this
Aquarius fellow,
This Eddie Linden?
Is he some sort
Of astronaut
In the bend of the wind
That the poor folks
Like us remember
Who did demons for us
As we struggled to climb
On to the empty page?

Good luck, so.

To the beat
Of your Irish
Sottish heart
From this upturned barrel
I send you
A drum of delight.

Cherry Blossom Again

Cherry blossom falls again
From the tree. Spring
Has drifted away and old age
Drags around me.
Why did sense pass me by
Without a primrose of recognition?

Will I never emerge from the reel
Of the ring, till the enchanted earth
Smiles cynically?
Will the mist always hide the garden from me?

Old People's Outing: Ageism

The old man on the telly
At the old people's outing
Was smiling but not breathing.
He was dressed in women's clothes.

The compère had dressed all the old men
In women's clothes,
Rolled up their pants to expose
Their soiled long-johns.
Fun, they yelled loudly.
This is real fun, they cackled
To keep the shudder of death away
But the one old man
Smiled hopelessly.
He had, for the last time,
Made a fool of himself.

Block

To beat the block
She painted dried flowers,
Baked bread,
Put wine in the Borsch,
Read *Finnegans Wake*,
But still her mind was as flat as Hungary.
'I need to fall in love,
I need pain,' she cried,
'Real pain.
Not just bad news on the telephone.'

The Lady Who Went on Strike Outside The Iveagh Hostel Because of its Early Closing Hours

I am Lily, comfy, leave
Me alone. My daft umbrellas
Shelter me. My mattress
Shapes my bones.

You can have old pin-
Stripe and his lock-up
Face in the Iveagh.

Why should I snuff
His candle light
And blow his dandelion clock?
The Liberties is my domain.
My carpet runs from Thomas Street
To St. Nicholas Without.

I lie here from Monday to Sunday.
My street's my Alphabet Walk.
I have a god-room
On this leaning street and
Love on my tree like ivy.
I am Lily, comfy, live or die.

Ghost Child Runs

The top of my house succumbed to fire,
Slates lie where they fell,
A bay window at the side
Swings on one hinge
Like the tongue of a famine child.
The room I slept in staggers
Under the ceiling-weight of rubble.
I can feel the noise of masonry settling
As the fire raced through its innards –
With casualties of floor
And ceiling, joist and window frame.

I burrow through basement
And drawing room – cyclamen wallpaper
Shrouds my shoulders or falls dog-eared
Into folds of heavy dust.
Two bats flash past – a spitting sound,
The radar of childhood quickens.

Going back (home) after forty years
May be a mistake, for now
The tall bay horse, coat dark as wine,
Stands, straddle-legged on the gravel.
A short walk to the spent wood
That runs crooked into the stream
Beyond Durkin's yard … The tall horse
Stamps its unshod hooves
Like gloved hands knocking
On the powdery wood
Of the old hall door. Mr. Durkin
Too, is long long dead – a man for books,

No time to tie his laces
Or straighten his aching back.
Ghost horse, ghost man, ghost child runs.

The Grave-digger

He came, saying
'Keep it Country',
Clint Eastwood riding
The stacks. 'It smells sweet
Up here in the cemetery.'

He said, 'Neighbour,
I'm country,
And that's the seventh dug.
It's a bad November.'

He came into the pit,
Earth and all. They took
The mule-train fast
The wires zinged,
A gorse fire raged.
'No putting it out
In this class of wind
Though it's from the West and sweet.'

Morning she heard the horse
Shake its bit, the harness clang.
She wondered about the sea,
Would the star-cold water
Suffice to cool her thighs?

A Paean for My Uncle Kit Who Died Before I Was Born

What did you think of
All those years
Pegging away in the mines?

Just a little short of breath,
you wrote, a touch of miner's
phthisis, nothing much

after seven years below.
Many men die after three,
that's what you wrote

from Benoni, Transvaal
in 1917 and three years later,
you were dead.

The price of diamonds fell,
And you all went out on strike
What was it? A drunken brawl?

Did you hit your head
On the edge of the pavement?
Did someone say:

'What's he doing there
Lying in the muck?'
An old young man of thirty-five,

Why did you go to Africa to die?
What did they tell you, your family?
That you were too wild

Too dangerously wild
For their Protestant
Mores? Too eccentric?

Did you tell them, 'So I'll go
Seek my fortune elsewhere
If I'm a nuisance here.'

The Black sheep dragging
The family down,
Did you embarrass them

With your curly locks
So beautifully portrayed
By Orpen when you were a boy.

You were full of wonder then,
As later you must have been
All those years so far from home,

Those seven long years
In the dark African tunnels,
Wondering what brought you there.

But you took your wonder with you
Nearly as far as man can go
And closed the book on it.

They didn't write to you.
They tore up all your letters.
Only a single one survived.

You were my favourite uncle
Although we never met.
Your face plays on the lute

Of my imagination,
The one friend out of all
I might have had.

The Ballad of the Fisherman's Wife

She brushed the salty weeping from her cheekbones,
Thrown by the feathered heaving of the spray.
She stubbed her toe against the herring boxes.
Death is different, it keeps away.

The silver dropped from beaks of flying seagulls,
The swell is rising. Someone ought to say
That harbour symbols cause a crazy freedom
And death is different, it keeps away,

An empty sack! She wandered off
Back to her semi-detached along the quay.
Her rage subsided like over-watered flowers.
Death is different, it keeps away.

Parchment fingers printed against the window.
'The boat is late,' she whispered, 'Keep away.'
'But I'll come in and prove that nothing alters
Death. It's different, it keeps away."

She took the 'Foreign Missions' from the dresser.
She took a fiver out of last week's pay.
'Bring bread and wine and spirits, then,' she ordered.
'Death is different, it keeps away.'

Innocents

In B-movies
They use tomato ketchup.
In art films
They use expensive
Cosmetic paint,
Not even obtainable in Ireland.

In real life
They use blood.

Bag Lady

I knew her when she was a bag lady.
She trundled places like the North Circular Road,
O'Connell Street and Fairview,
Followed the Liffey, a restless bone,
Lay down under the lid of Clery's.
But when she knew the eyes of the orphans
Had left her, she folded her briefcase
And took the long dark highway
That had always beckoned.

Barnacles

Irish Sea north westerly 7 or 8
Increasing 10 for a time
Shannon Rockall northerly
Increasing north backing northwest
Dogger Cromarty Viking
Malin Hebrides.
Doors bang, buckets race
Down the field, my skirt
Wraps round me
Like a sari. Gulls lift
And scatter like paper.
A boat bobs like a bead
As a shoulder lifts
And rolls in with a shrug.
And then the thrash of wings.
It is six o'clock, the island calls,
And the geese face into the gale,
A cardiograph in the sky …

Insomnia

With me in my truckle bed
There is a hound
A hound in my head
There is no gainsaying it
It howls

It is the lessons of darkness

Oh Couperin
Couperin Le Grand

Pigeon Outside the Dead Woman's House

Like a casual passer-by
She strolls, her shawl
Of feathers neatly pinned.

Outside Theresa's cottage
She picks at the crumbs
Of the old woman's soul.

Maybe takes it on loan.
When life peters out like that
There's no certainty

Of who is who, whether
Theresa is the pigeon
Or the pigeon is Theresa.

It is true that Theresa,
When still living,
Gazed at the island,

The island of her birth
Perhaps thinking
Were I a bird

I'd give it a peck,
A peck of a kiss,
Just there and back.

So maybe the pigeon
Is just hanging around
For instructions.

Maugherow Movements

He repeated the word *Duvet*
As though it were a charm.
Duvet, he said, curling his socks
Around her feet.

The Invisible, from the USA to Iraq

We are too late again.
We have to get our bearings
In the gutter.

The sky is dark.
The birds assemble –
A murder of crows.

We dream of justice
Where a pride of lawyers
Tumbles through our brains.

We must take action, we say,
Against the invisible.
It thinks it has us trapped.

It likes to set pipebombs
For unsuspecting children
As it shouts out loudly:

'She's only a girl-woman
Crying on the sofa.'

The Song of the Whale

And the whale beached
In Lislarry. And they brought the JCB
And buried it. All thirty foot of it.
They said it was black,
Shining skin from the sea.
Grey blue, some argued
All thirty foot of it.
And the whale men came,
They came all the way from Cork,
For that is where the whale men
And the dolphin men hang out,
And they made their notes
And ecological plans and took
Blood samples and measured the tide
So that the whale now lies
Under the limestone reaches,
Proud steps to the summer storm,
Turquoise and shimmering,
Great sea mammal, partner of song.

We Sell, You Buy: Gulf War 1

We sell, you buy:
Exocet, Pershing, Cruise, what odds?
We sell, you buy.

We have reasons a-plenty, piled up like pillows
On the creaking bed of your desire
To see the earth crack like an egg
And pour itself into the empty cup of space.
We sell, you buy.

The world's on the H.P spiral.
If we make black snow we must distribute.
Sales distribution, input, output,
That's the name of the game.

Why can't you understand, you of feeble
Belief: 'That man can't possibly do this?'
Of course you'll purchase the brand new sun
That'll give you a tan without flying south
For the price you're prepared to give –
Freedom was the word I think you mentioned?

I once read a book about some old Jap
Who saw the shadow of his daughter on a wall.
By the corkscrew of fate he survived to tell the tale,
Went far away and cultivated carp.

S.A.D.

> *Winter is icummen in,*
> *Lhude sing Goddamm*
> — Ezra Pound

The swallows pack up
And go.
Tomorrow the geese
Will come.
Inside the house
In the purple dark
The table
With its city of junk
Tells you
That winter leans on you,
Has nudged you through all
The tower and babel
Of the past months
When a kind of summer
Was. Now the table tells you
It's the S.A.D.
Stale bread, hard as a helmet,
Dregs of tea, the last teabag
Like a dead mouse,
Yesterday's
Half-finished crossword,
Tells you
It's for winter.

Who's for winter?
Says your man
Below, growing his house.

The Horse Protestant Joke is Over

There's a small church
By the Big House
Outside of which
The notice reads
Everyone welcome.

Two grinning
Millionaires
Have bought the Big House

And they will have horses,
And they will have jeeps,
And maybe ride rough-shod
Over the parishioners
Of the little church
Which says
Everyone welcome.

House for Sale

for Sophia McColgan

Still the house stands
In its rope of wind,
Small cenotaph
To the weeds of evil,
The stone of memory
A solid fortress
That time
Will not erase.

The children's voices
Under chair and wardrobe,
Between the cracks
In the lino …
The broken hinge of terror
In the swinging door
That swings over and over
Is the house's destiny

Till it crumbles in history
Unwanted, unsold.

Song

I gave a poem to my friend.
He spat upon the burning ground.
I said, *My friend, it's not the end,*
My song is better than it sounds.
But he said lately he had found
That matter divulged and matter penned
Created enemies all around.

I wrapped my poem up in lead
And threw it in his scarlet face.
I said, *My friend, I wish you dead*
For such a terrible disgrace.
But then he only laughed instead
And wrapped his Easter up in lace.

In the Out-Patients of St. Mary's Hospital, On the Eve of Good Friday Last

High on Reds, short for Seconal,
Drunk out of her person,
bumming fags – beautiful lady
of London wept for the crucified Lord.
He died for us, for me, for you,
Transfigured, tomorrow we'll toast Him with whiskey.
The casualty's slack lips tightened.
Her words, encrusted with slime and sentiment,
Banged the air like a fist.
She wept. She crossed herself.
Tears from her crazy Calvary –
The prescription got would rise again
In Wigmore Street –
The all-night drug-addicts' haven.
Perfection is easily gained.
Social Security pays – legal high,
Suicide, bets on the Derby – you name it.
She was foul-mouthed, loving and highly practical.

'The Act of Poetry Is a Rebel Act'
—*Michael Hartnett*

Possibly those inquisitive eyes
Grasped the horizon
Of his wonder gift,
Tell-tales of lift-the-heart
Follies – like addressing the statue
In Kiltimagh of a brandy-shadowed
Morning: *No wars of mercy fought
On his behalf.* His waging, lonesome
As any poet's, playing the poker
Of 'See you, raise you' till its echo tumbled
From the kitty of common sense.
How well he knew
'The act of poetry
Is a rebel act.'

Precisely

Of course
All things are rich to me.
Precision, equally, is correct.
The muscles of a boy's back
In early Latin sun,
The line of a Bentley tourer
Parked in a Georgian square,
Not to mention the neck
Of a racehorse,
Money itself,
The ablative absolute,
White in the sun,
The cold of a cathedral,
The smell of a new tennis ball,
Couperin's *Leçons de Ténebrè* ...

Still, I have seen
The boy, the Bentley
And the racehorse.
I have felt money and the cold
Of a cathedral,
Have smelled the new tennis ball
And heard Couperin's
Leçons de Ténebrè.

But memory games
Make patches wear
In the heart.

Prison Poem III

for a friend doing life in Portlaoise

I walk the crazy paving, the path of lies,
The micro-chip of satisfaction,
And mingle with the funny-money men
Who gossip on the shoulders of the judges,
But I think of you between the intervals of pacing
Or silence as on the edge of circumstance.

And with twice and nothing of what they have,
The bastards.

I send you the white bird of attendance,
The swallow that left too soon, migrated South,
The simplicities of daisies under boots.

Remember Jean-Paul Sartre and other soldiers of fortune
Who lived on the rim of existence and survived
The cinder that drops beneath the grate and stays alight,
The fish that lies beneath the shadow of the stone.

Prison Poem IV

written during The Hunger Strike, 1980

I do so want to live but my body,
Stringent in its monkey martyrdom,
Withdraws into shadow splendour.
It knows I am helpless now to order it.

In effect the delay in dying spreads
Flat and reflective as a mirror.
Voices of others at one remove
Deploy old friends, natives of my mind.
They argue, frustrate me with their insistence.

It's hard to see: motes of light tumble
Like tadpoles. I remember chemistry,
A cross teacher, the jargon of formulae,
How all could be clarified in the body-mortal
If only I paid attention.

Some days I am careless; I cope adequately
With skin and thighs. Feet, more determined,
Claim my attention as though
They braved the frontier without permit.
This amuses me. I admire them for their stress
Of personality. Allow them to peer from beneath
Their triangle of blanket. I would like to meet them half-way,
Acknowledge that their geometry is relevant.

On other days I am invaded by heat, my skull especially.
In this state my mind is laid back
For the repeated information of pain.
I do so want to live
Or is that someone else talking?

Dublin, December 1980

Two Poems i.m. Stevie Smith

THE GIRL IN A BOX

Once upon a time
There was a girl in a box
And her pretty china face
Was full of love.
(She never moved.)

*Why does she lie there like that
Without moving, so frail, so spent?*

Perhaps she is dead, they said.
And away they went.

DEAR MR. PSYCHIATRIST

Dear Mr. Psychiatrist
I don't like your pills.
(I prefer my ills)

I am a doll's house
And my bricks are ruby red.
Mummy and Daddy are in my bottles
With pretty plastic phials of love.

Oh, sweet rainbow, break me.

The Bed Bug

I am a bed bug.
I am flat.
I am starving.

They say God didn't invent me
But I am alive.
Society has done for me.
I live in a matchbox.

Somebody invented me,
If not God,
So I can live indefinitely
In a matchbox
Alone.

I am alive
But they won't feed me.
I am transparent
But basically
I am a bed bug.

In My Darling Liza's Eyes

In my darling Liza's eyes
I see her father.
Her shoulders are square, like his,
As though she carried two buckets
On a yoke.

She leans over the bar and slurps her vodka.
Oh, Liza, do you hear that voice in your throat?

Four Woodbines

In the torn and dirty sheets of those winter years
Spent in my wet mac, clutching the green packet
With its fiery orange sash – four Woodbines –
And my mongrel dog scratching its pedigree of fleas,
I was happy as a child could be, hiding under the shelf of Confey.

Drunk from the spilling rain, the stumpy field
Shrank from the ruined church, the glue factory,
Four headstones, I remember, aslant and broken as winos.

The winter mists came early then,
Tucked up the river in a long white scarf

While, heavy with fish and water-hens,
It rolled on quietly in the textured night.

Two-pence halfpenny – old money –
Not much to pay in retrospect
For the healing wonder of that glorious leaf.

Mrs. Katherine Dunne, Street Trader, Camden Street, Dublin, Died March 1983

Three on the bottle! Just like me!
She gave me a pram then – did she remember?
Now I address her dignity – summer and winter,
On the pavements of time. One day, too,
And I cold, she gave me tea as she stood
With snow on her lips and the shyest of smiles.

But that was a while ago now and the children
Have plagued and played us, as tombola and fife.
The bingo of life picks the strangest numbers
And drums up tunes in the weirdest disarray.

In the lamplight of chat – how the country swings
(and not for us) – I'd finger the aubergines,
The wounded cabbages, the French Delicious,
Tasteless as electricity in their super-shine,
Happy to find an Irish Cox
Whose sweet juice runs on the tongue
And she'd say: *Ah, I kept that one for you.*

Not easy to be a trader all those years,
Summer and winter, watching the generations pass
Like camels on a video horizon,
And staying motionless as Asia, never growing old
Herself, just wiser and more beautiful.

Was she always waiting for that pain to come,
To call a taxi like a tumbril and say *Cheerio*

And see you soon. I wonder why I'm left
The simple pride of having known her.

If the Baby Powers we shared
In the rush and tinsel of one Christmas Eve
May not be drunk this year nor any future
Year, I'll gladly hold the gift-horse bridle reins
And wait for the pain to come to call a cab.

Nightmare

It is dark in my father's shoe,
His experienced shoe. I scratch my skin
On the buckle and the laces.

He crunches about
On top of me. Underneath his arm

He has a cricket bat.
He is waiting
For the next man out.

A Mother Mourns Her Heroin-Addicted Daughter

How could I have dreamt
That my bird of paradise,
My green-clad hippie girl,
Could be so reduced
To the gammon face of poverty,
The incessant whinge of a child.

If we rolled up time like a ball
I'd give you the cherries of my nipples,
I'd wash you almond clean
And lay your hair like lint
On the cartilege of my breast.

A prey to the barren street, you're lost
On the breach of years that no silk
Nor cotton drawing-to of threads
Can mend. The void. Your path is marked
Like gull-prints on an empty beach.

The drug has perished your will.
You float like a stick on a pond
In here, in there – to a harbour of lily-trees,
Or held for days in scum till the light
Breeze lifts you and you edge along.

Will you walk on my street once more?
I'll raise my pavements to keep you safe,
Open the balcony of my arms.

I will buckle your shoes again
And shine the mirror for your dance.

But you will not throw away your bag of tricks.
Your monkey fingers cling to the safety net
In which you nightly land, having walked
The trembling wire and heard the screams
Of anticipation, seen the up-turned mouths.

How can we meet down the glaciers
Of days, the furnaces of nights?

The Violets of the Poor

My muse invites me to forget my debts,
Pile up more enemies.

Invoke the few

Who are helpful, generous
But not always honest.
To make secrets for the few
Like "whispering time".

But the few are filtered
And numbered in the funerals.
They follow the coffins.

So I pacify my muse
By joining the cortège
And sprinkling my secrets to the mourners
Like the violets of the poor.

Black in Achill

What makes black so black?
Black soul, black Protestant
Black widow, black cat,
Black holes, black death.
So many blacks in Achill:
Dugort, Dooagh, Dooega
Dookinella. Black field,
Black land, black plain.
But what if, like a camera click,
The sun comes out
And shadows sythe
The mountain's umber skin
And gorse-gold sand?

Megan Fair Remembered, 1977

for Jacky and my three sons, Nicky, Eddie and Johnny

Crosslegged, she sits, the pregnant one,
Her boyfriend beside her. The flame of pride
Illuminates the cushion of his cheeks.
My sons throw frisbee beyond the circle of the camp,
A white knife skimming the shoulder of the field.
My daughter bends from me to whisper to the embers.
I finger the back of her hair, rising and falling.
Against the fire it is brighter than fire,
The colour of drenched apricot.
It ribs against my palm,
Electric, compelling.

In a pit, we have made this fire,
Scooped the crusted earth with our fingers
And lain criss-cross the twigs,
Ignited by sandwich wrappings, old newspaper,
Till the bronze flame entered the sides of the logs
And was comfortable, would work for us,
To make the grass a shade warmer for our thighs,
The skin tighten on our cheeks.

The children are fed first; my daughter
Has spread the cloth way back from the heat.
They are everywhere, like dark squirrels
Cupping their hands for the offerings she has to give.
Already the black pot bubbles – the soup slides quietly
Up the edges. Her limbs are loose and purposeful,
Her thoughts retain their cosmic pattern.

Now the fires are everywhere in the horn of night.
For a long time it was twilight,

A muslin of mist had clothed the landscape
But now the clusters of distant Lowry figures –
All at business with life –
Are at work, kindling carefully as we did,
Stitching rubies to the flank of the secret hill.

There is nothing to do now only wait
For the acres of feeling to be ploughed back into time,
A brief memory of others perhaps, the solid footsteps of strangers.
The Welsh, curious as bullocks about this Irish family
Or what we are wary of in the valley hidden below –
A suspicious village, a chapel crouching in its bed of meadowsweet,
Or the offering of the wine of oak leaves and mountain ash.

www.ingramcontent.com/pod-product-compliance
Lightning Source LLC
LaVergne TN
LVHW092049060526
838201LV00047B/1303